# Terrific Tongue Twisters

# Sola Printing

# HOW MANY TIMES CAN YOU REPEAT THESE TONGUE TWISTERS BEFORE GETTING MIXED UP?

# HOW FAST CAN YOU SAY THESE TOPSY TURVY TONGUE TWISTERS?

# IF A DOG CHEWS SHOES, WHOSE SHOES DOES HE CHOOSE?

# TOP CHOPSTICK SHOPS STOCK TOP CHOPSTICKS.

# SELFISH SHELLFISH.

NO NEED TO LIGHT A NIGHT-LIGHT ON A LIGHT NIGHT LIKE TONIGHT.

# THE GREAT GREEK GRAPE GROWERS GROW GREAT GREEK GRAPES.

LINDA-LOU LAMBERT
LOVES LEMON
LOLLIPOP LIPGLOSS.

# ROBERTA RAN RINGS AROUND THE ROMAN RUINS.

# HE THREW THREE FREE THROWS.

# A SYNONYM FOR CINNAMON IS A CINNAMON SYNONYM.

ONE-ONE WAS A RACE HORSE. TWO-TWO WAS ONE TOO. ONE-ONE WON ONE RACE. TWO-TWO WON ONE TOO.

# FRED FED TED BREAD AND TED FED FRED BREAD.

# SCISSORS SIZZLE,
# THISTLES SIZZLE.

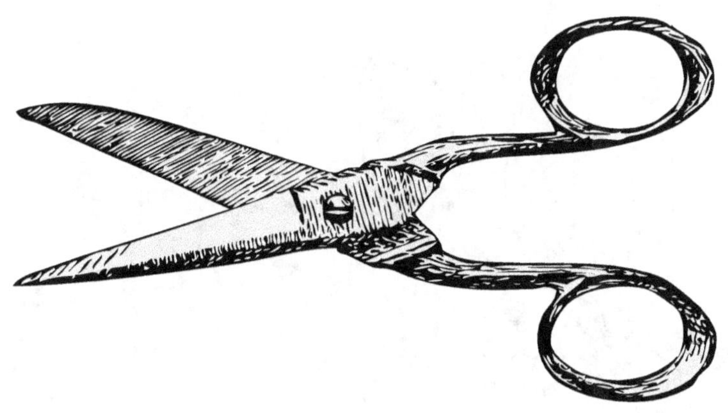

# BETTY'S BIG BUNNY BOBBLED BY THE BLUEBERRY BUSH.

# FOUR FURIOUS FRIENDS FOUGHT FOR THE PHONE.

# GOBBLING GARGOYLES GOBBLED GOBBLING GOBLINS.

# MANY AN ANEMONE SEES AN ENEMY ANEMONE.

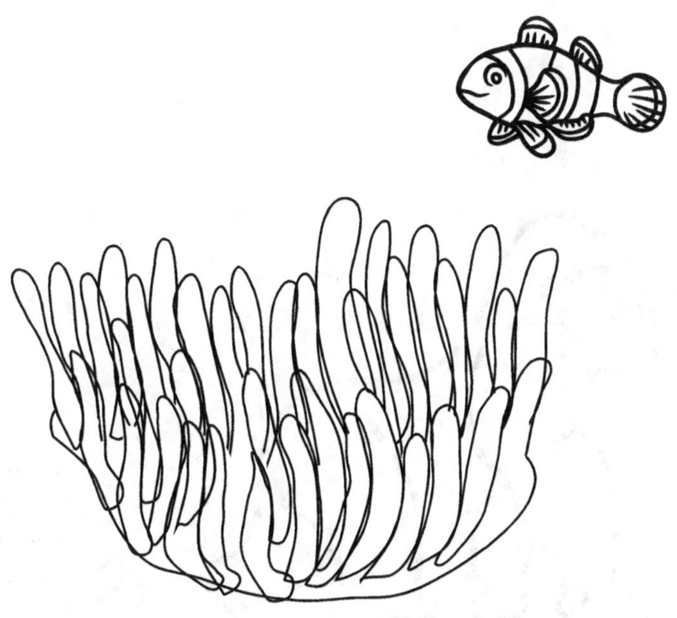

# AN APE HATES GRAPE CAKES.

I SAW A KITTEN EATING CHICKEN IN THE KITCHEN.

# SMELLY SHOES AND SOCKS SHOCK SISTERS.

# TIE TWINE TO THREE TREE TWIGS.

# FRESH FRENCH FRIED FRITTERS.

# BETTY BOUGHT BUTTER BUT THE BUTTER WAS BITTER, SO BETTY BOUGHT BETTER BUTTER TO MAKE THE BITTER BUTTER BETTER.

IF YOU MUST CROSS A COARSE CROSS COW ACROSS A CROWDED COW CROSSING, CROSS THE CROSS COARSE COW ACROSS THE CROWDED COW CROSSING CAREFULLY.

# SHE SELLS SEASHELLS BY THE SEASHORE.

# PETER PIPER PICKED A PECK OF PICKLED PEPPERS. HOW MANY PICKLED PEPPERS DID PETER PIPER PICK?

FUZZY WUZZY WAS A BEAR. FUZZY WUZZY HAD NO HAIR. FUZZY WUZZY WASN'T VERY FUZZY, WAS HE?

# HOW MUCH WOOD WOULD A WOODCHUCK CHUCK IF A WOODCHUCK COULD CHUCK WOOD?

# IF A BLACK BUG BLEEDS BLACK BLOOD, WHAT COLOR BLOOD DOES A BLUE BUG BLEED?

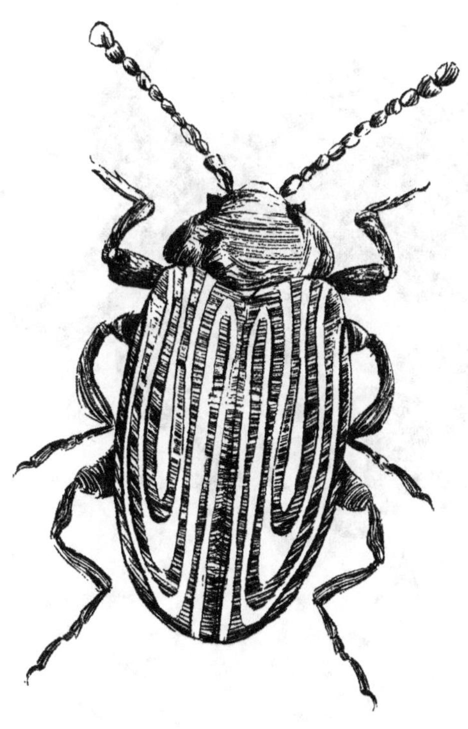

# IF TWO WITCHES WERE WATCHING TWO WATCHES: WHICH WITCH WOULD WATCH WHICH WATCH?

# DOES YOUR SPORTS SHOP STOCK SHORT SOCKS WITH SPOTS?

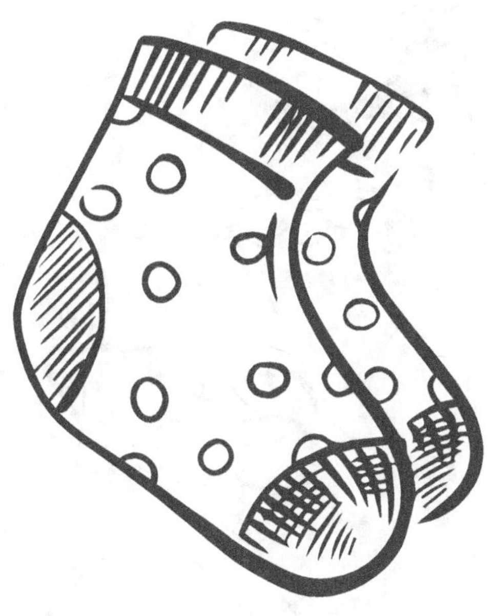

# MANY MUMBLING MICE ARE MAKING MERRY MUSIC IN THE MOONLIGHT.

# TWELVE TWINS TWIRLED TWELVE TWIGS.

# FIVE FRANTIC FROGS FLED FROM FIFTY FIERCE FISHES.

BETTY AND BOB
BROUGHT BACK BLUE
BALLOONS FROM THE
BIG BAZAAR.

# ZEBRAS ZIG AND ZEBRAS ZAG.

# FRED FED TED BREAD AND TED FED FRED BREAD.

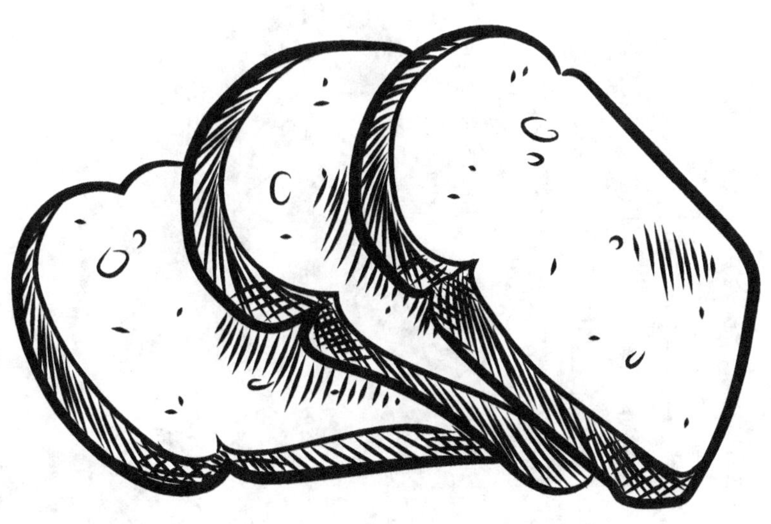

# TOY BOAT. TRY BOAT.
# TOY BOAT. TRY BOAT.

# A BIG BLACK BUG BIT A BIG BLACK BEAR.

# SHEEP SHOULD SLEEP IN A SHED.

# CHESTER CHEETAH CHEWS A CHUNK OF CHEAP CHEDDAR CHEESE.

# SIX SLEEK SWANS SWAM SWIFTLY SOUTHWARDS.

# BOUNCING BED BUGS BORROWED BLANKETS.

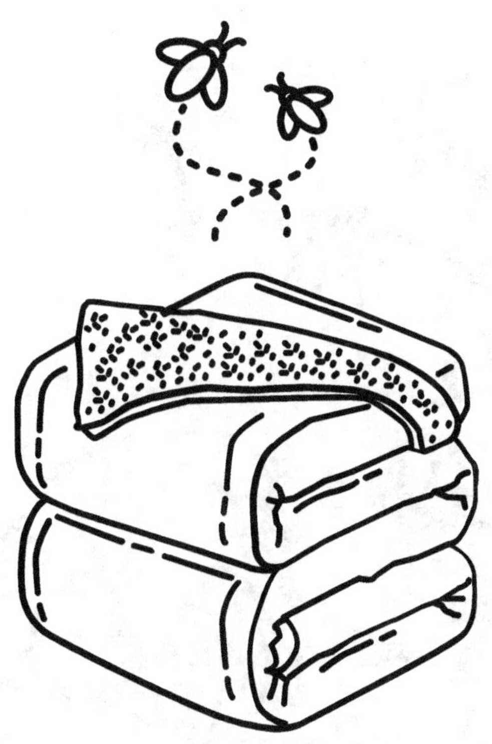

# BABOON BAMBOO.
# BABOON BAMBOO.

# A HAPPY HIPPO HOPPED AND HICCUPPED.

# IF PRACTICE MAKES PERFECT AND PERFECT NEEDS PRACTICE, I'M PERFECTLY PRACTICED AND PRACTICALLY PERFECT.

# A SNAKE SNEAKS TO SEEK A SNACK.

# KITTY CAUGHT THE KITTEN IN THE KITCHEN.

# BAD MONEY, MAD BUNNY.

FRESH FRIED FISH, FISH FRESH FRIED, FRIED FISH FRESH, FISH FRIED FRESH.

WHETHER THE WEATHER IS WARM, WHETHER THE WEATHER IS HOT, WE HAVE TO PUT UP WITH THE WEATHER, WHETHER WE LIKE IT OR NOT.

SHE SEES CHEESE.

SHE SEES CHEESE.

# FOUR FINE FRESH FISH FOR YOU.

# COOKS COOK
# CUPCAKES QUICKLY.

# A BIG BLACK BEAR SAT ON A BIG BLACK RUG.

# RORY'S LAWN RAKE RARELY RAKES REALLY RIGHT.

# WE SURELY SHALL SEE THE SUNSHINE SOON.

FOUR FRANTIC FLIES
FLED FROM FIFTY
FIERCE FROGS.

# EACH EASTER EDDIE EATS EIGHTY EASTER EGGS.

# WILLY'S REAL REAR WHEEL.

# A SNAKE SNEAKS TO SEEK A SNACK.

# SIX CZECH CRICKET CRITICS.

# SPECIFIC PACIFIC.
# SPECIFIC PACIFIC.

# TOMMY TOSSED HIS TWELFTH TOOTH.

# GREEN GLASS GLOBES
# GLOW GREENLY.

# I HAVE GOT A DATE AT A QUARTER TO EIGHT: I'LL SEE YOU AT THE GATE, SO DON'T BE LATE.

BOBBY BIPPY BOUGHT
A BAT. BOBBY BIPPY
BOUGHT A BALL. WITH
HIS BAT, BOB BANGED
THE BALL.

# WAYNE WENT TO WATCH WALRUSES.

# A SLIMY SNAKE SLITHERED THROUGH THE SANDY SAHARA.

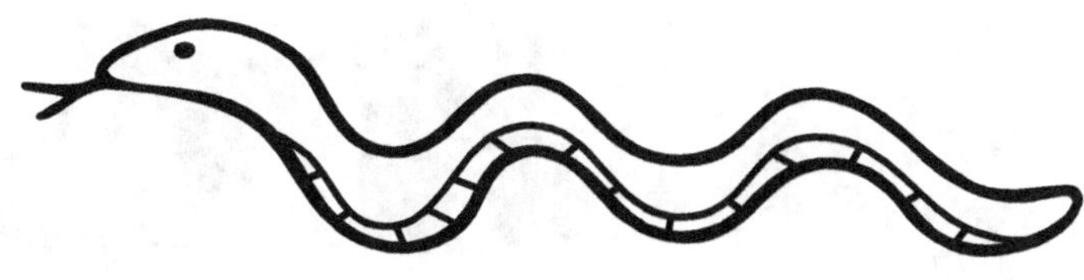

# SO, THIS IS THE SUSHI CHEF.

# STUPID SUPERSTITION!

STUPID SUPERSTITION!

# SINGING SALLY SANG SONGS ON SINKING SAND.

TWO TINY TIGERS TAKE
TWO TAXIS TO TOWN.

# I WISH FOR A FISH
# IN MY DISH.

SHE SEES CHEESE.

SHE SEES CHEESE.

SHE SEES CHEESE.

# THE PIRATES' PRIVATE PROPERTY.

# Read More From Sola Printing!

## Fun Riddles For Bright Kids

## Hilarious Classroom Jokes For Kids